AF723804

BOB ZAHN

S LAB
L ONLINESS
A TONEMENT
B EAUTY
C OPS
I NSANITY
T EQUILA
Y OUTHFULNESSAGAIN

— 'Zeigh', Transient (Cover)

www.bobzahn.com

AMERICAN GOTHIC REVISITED: SLAB CITY—THE LAST FREE PLACE IN AMERICA

Portfolio by **Bob Zahn**

Interview by **Julia Dean**

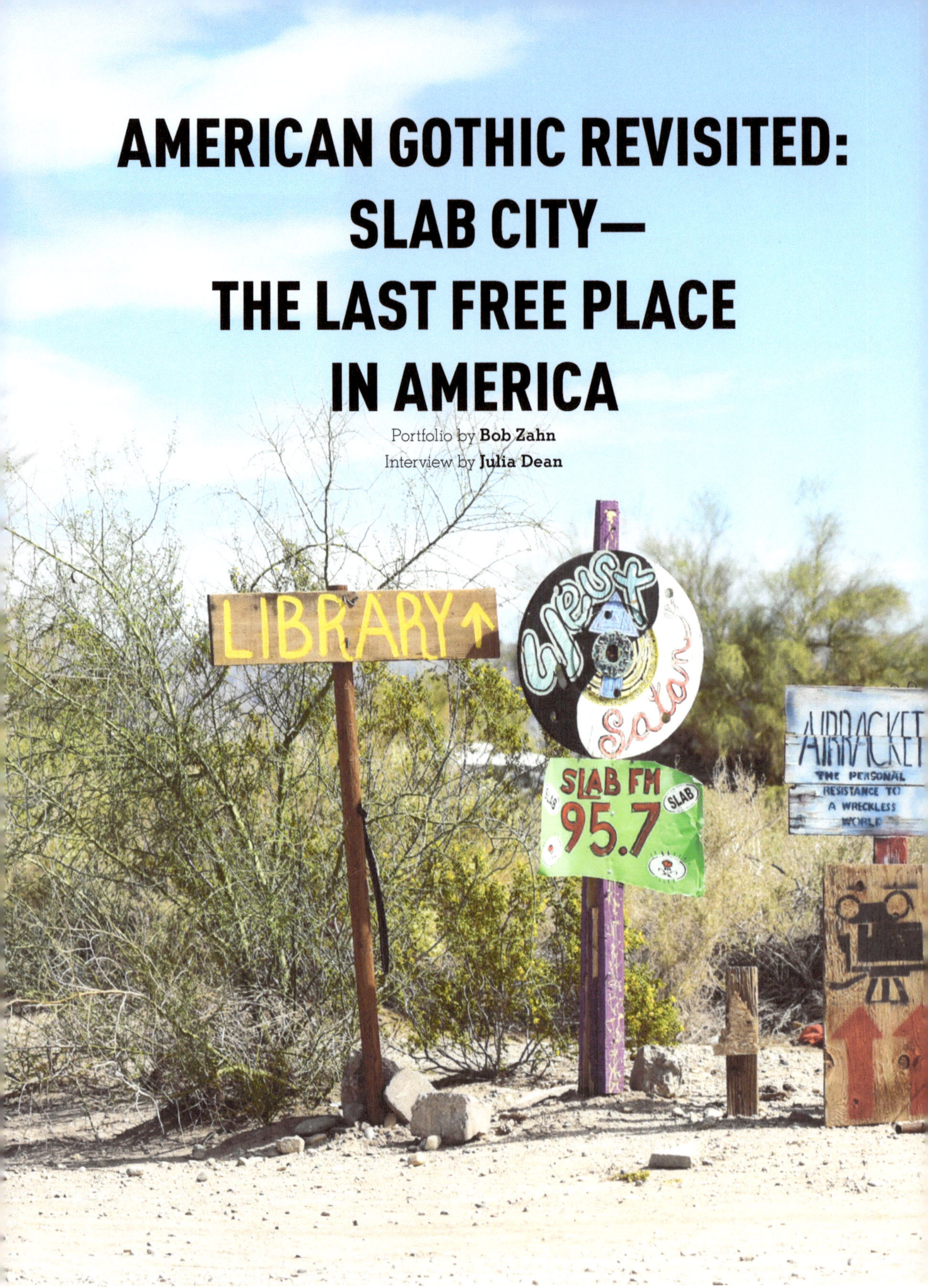

Low Road (Loaner on Wheels) sign posts

"THERE'S A TWO-LANE HIGHWAY THROUGH SLAB CITY. THE LAND IS FLAT AND 126 FEET BELOW SEA LEVEL. YOU CAN SEE THE STARS AT NIGHT. PEOPLE ARE HONEST AND REAL. THIS IS A TOTAL CHANGE IN MY LIFESTYLE, AND I WANTED IT."

— BOB ZAHN

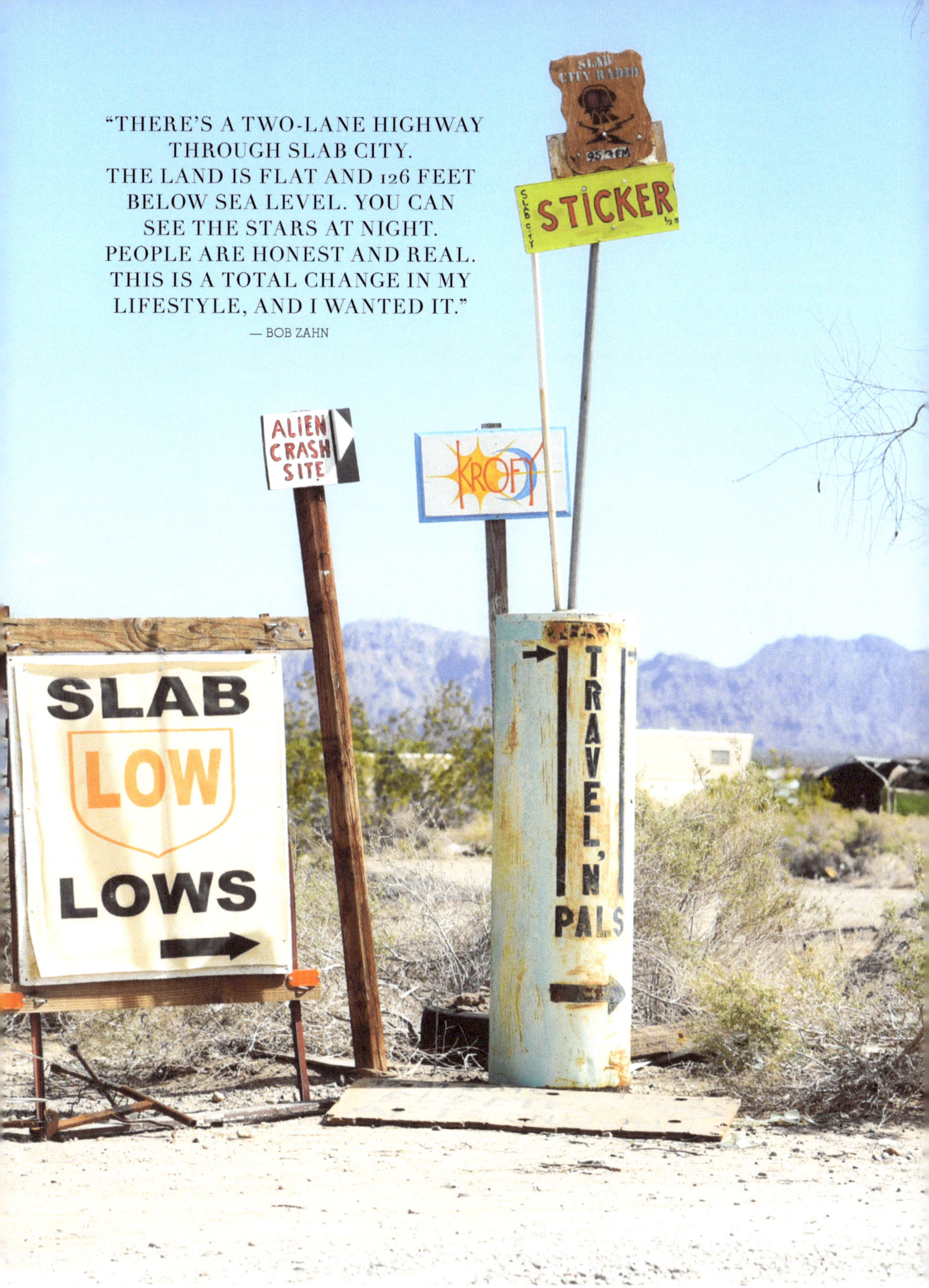

When Bob Zahn showed me his latest fine art photography collection, American Gothic Revisited: Slab City—The Last Free Place In America, *I looked at him and said, "America needs to see this." Slab City is in the Sonoran Desert in California. According to Wikipedia, it "is used by recreational vehicle owners and squatters from across North America." Because the temperatures in the summer can easily reach 120 degrees, only around 150 people live there year round. They choose to live there mostly due to poverty, to learn to live off the grid or simply just to be left alone. There is no electricity, running water, sewers or garbage removal.*

Zahn was drawn to these residents from the minute he discovered Slab City.

"I LOVE TO GIVE, AND WHAT I COULD GIVE PEOPLE WAS A PORTRAIT OF THEMSELVES. IT FELT VERY INTIMATE. I ENJOYED THAT ENORMOUSLY."

— BOB ZAHN

He gained their trust by making visits with his camera. In 2014, he moved to Calipatria, a town of 7,095 residents just 13 miles away from Slab City. There is no better way to document a place than to be in the middle of it, which Zahn has done for several years now. The project is far from over.

This body of work is a true documentation of a unique American place. The portraits are real, and the words meaningful. Zahn talks to each person at length about why they choose to live in Slab City. Take a look. Something in this body of work is bound to move you.

Julia Dean: What led you to photography and how long have you been doing it?

Bob Zahn: I've been involved in the arts since I was six years old, and I'm a visual thinker. At 18 I got my first camera, then at 20 I bought my first Nikon, and that started it all. I've always been a portrait photographer for many reasons, but basically as I went to film school at New York University I realized that the close-up is the most important part of the movie. How you take that close-up really reflects on the person and the story.

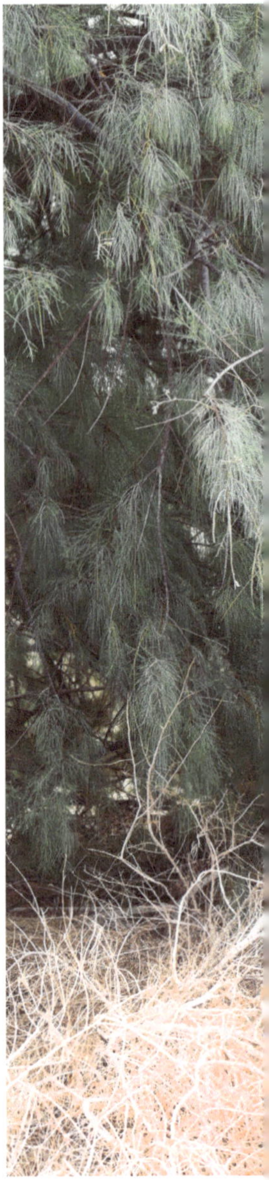

I was at NYU during the era when Martin Scorsese was a teacher and Oliver Stone was a student. And I saw incredible clashes between the two of them because he was just back from Vietnam and Marty was not into that whatsoever, but I could see *Platoon* and *Wall Street* right there in class.

JD: Wow, that is amazing. From film school then, did you proceed to have a career in film?

BZ: The last day of registration for my senior year, I received a rejection letter from the American Film Institute (AFI) as a film fellow, and there was a job that became available in the industry at a very famous rental house. So I had a choice: go back to school for only liberal arts classes, since I had taken all of the film classes, or there was a job. So I took the job. I began working for a company, eventually running their video department and progressing through there. I saw so many things about to come in the future but also saw so many things they were doing wrong, so I took the opportunity to start my own company in 1980.

JD: How do you identify as a photographer?

BZ: I'm a portrait photographer. I also tell stories with my photographs. So I would describe myself as somewhere between a portrait photographer and a documentary photographer.

JD: Did any one photographer or one moment or one time in history spark your interest in photography?

BZ: Well, this is what is so unusual: the answer is no. But I love to give, and what I could give people was a portrait of themselves. It felt very intimate. I enjoyed that enormously.

JD: Speaking of intimate, all our lives as photographers we've always looked through the camera. Someone looks back into the camera and you have that very special moment between you. Even though there's a camera in between you, you still feel it, and you're waiting for this great, candid moment to happen. How do you feel about taking pictures with a digital camera,

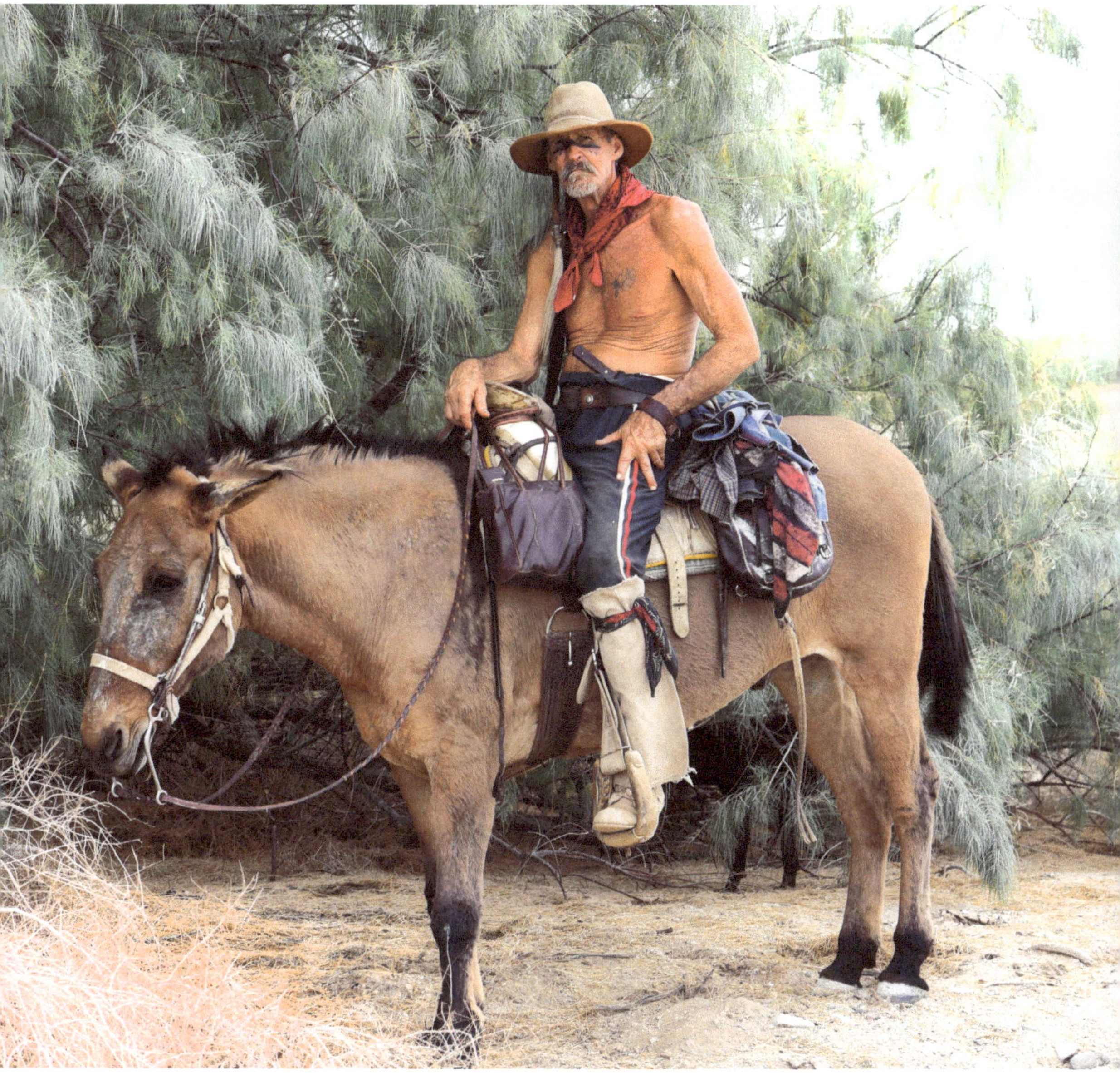

'Cuervo' and his mule 'Rock an' Roll', Suburbanite Slabbers, *"I've got to get back to nature. Civilization has left us nowhere."*

where you have to look at the back of the camera and they're looking at the front. Do you find that more difficult?

BZ: Richard Avedon used to use a camera where he would be able to look at the person directly. But I definitely need to look through the lens. The lens allows me to compose the photograph, and behind it is where I come alive.

JD: You said you're also a storyteller within your portraits. What kind of stories do you like to tell?

BZ: One of the first stories I did was about street performers in New York City. It was called *Street Performers Playing for Free*. It was all black and white, on Tri X 400. This was in the mid-seventies when I was going to NYU. It was such a free time in New York, and these were performers out in the streets doing wonderful things for whoever was walking by and for whatever money they wanted to give. The variety of performers was incredible: from steel pianists to guitarists, mind readers, mimes, dancers, jazz groups, jugglers. On the weekends, I would take my camera, and this would fill my spirit. There was a story there. Nobody has really seen it, but it was very diverse. That was my first documentary story.

Later on, I made a documentary film about the village where I lived, Hastings-on-Hudson, titled: *The Miracle on the Waterfront* because there was a level two toxic waste site right on the Hudson River, and we were trying to reclaim it. In between those two, all the students at NYU at the time got together and made a film called *Street Scenes* (1970). It was basically about the strikes on Wall Street and the clashes between the students and the Iron Steel Workers. Martin Scorsese was the director of that picture, and it went to the New York Film Festival. But there's only one copy of that film. We don't know where it is. It was just a wonderful time when we came together and, instead of protesting, made a film.

JD: Let's talk a little bit about *American Gothic Revisited* and Slab City, California. Can you tell me more about the project, the place and the people you've become so fond of?

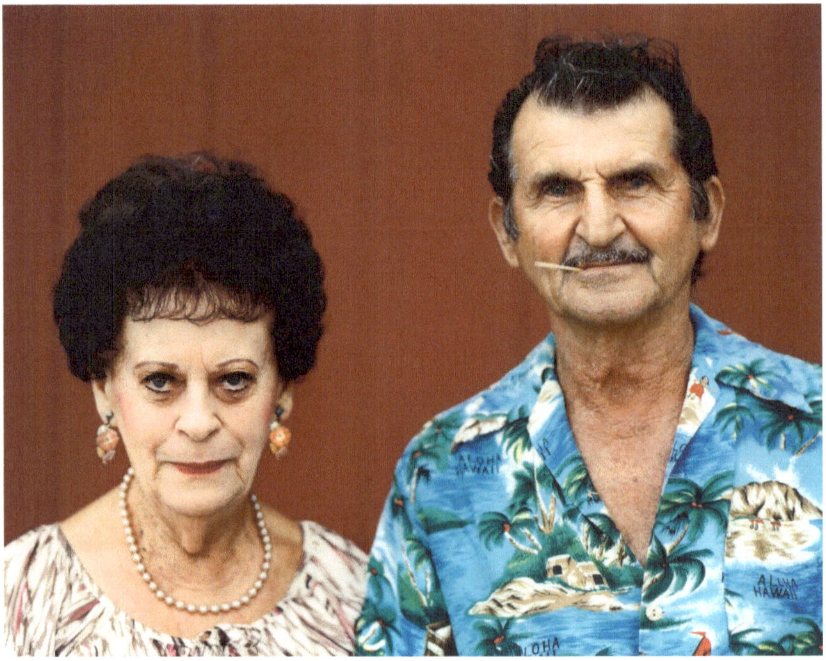

American Gothic II

BOB ZAHN
Photographer and documentarian Bob Zahn relocated from New York City to Calipatria, California to pursue his series *American Gothic Revisited*, which focuses on the people and landscape of nearby Slab City. Zahn studied film at NYU and participated in the making of *Street Scenes* (1970) with director Martin Scorsese. From 1980-2010, Zahn owned Broadcast Video Rentals in New York. Zahn has written, produced and directed his own films, including *Miracle on the Waterfront*.

JULIA DEAN
Julia Dean is a photographer, educator and the executive director and founder of the Los Angeles Center of Photography. She began her career as an apprentice to pioneering photographer Berenice Abbott and as a photo editor for the Associated Press. She has traveled to more than 45 countries freelancing for numerous relief groups and magazines and now concentrates on street photography. She is the author and photographer of the award-winning children's book, *A Year on Monhegan Island*.

SLAB CITY
An off-the-grid community in California's Sonoran Desert, Slab City is 156 miles northeast of San Diego and miles east of the Salton Sea. Slab City is both decommissioned and uncontrolled, and its population varies from about 150 more permanent residents in summer to several thousands of 'snowbirds' in winter. The site derives its name from concrete slabs that remain from the abandoned WWII Marine barracks of Camp Dunlap.

BZ: I took a photo of a couple at a roadside restaurant in Quartzsite, Arizona. I was having a meal at the restaurant when I saw them at the next booth, and my eyes bulged. When they were leaving, I literally ran after them and asked if I could take their portrait. That became the basis for this collection. I needed more compelling faces. Where would I find them? That was my question.

I saw Sean Penn's *Into the Wild*. For a few minutes it went to Salvation Mountain and Slab City, and I got an idea of what was there. So that was the direction I took. The first time I got to Slab City, I found Cuervo and his mule Rock 'n' Roll. When I took that picture, I knew I had found my location. There was an incredible story here. Incredible people. Incredible faces. So I started in February of 2014 and have been going back ever since. Now I live closeby—13 miles away.

JD: And you moved to be closer to your project?

BZ: Absolutely. I have become part of the community and am known as 'Foto Bob.' Throughout that entire period, I would take portraits of people. And that comes through. I'm not putting on any airs. I'm just letting the people flow through the lens. I try to be transparent. I don't want to put myself in there, but I want them to reveal themselves. I specifically ask them to look directly into the camera lens. For the audience, as they move left or right, forward or back, the subject's eyes are always on them. Their eyes are so expressive. I wanted people to see them as they were.

JD: How and where do these people live?

BZ: Basically, they live in tents or old trailer homes, the largest is 52' long, with a large capacity water tank outside, commercial grade dc batteries, inverters, a bedroom, bathroom, kitchen, air conditioner. Some have televisions. Slab City's been called off the grid because there's no electricity, no running water and no sewage. There's electricity from solar power and water is brought in. There are just outhouses, no sewage treatment. This is a very, very unusual lifestyle. The summer temperatures can get to be as high as 120° F.

The true Slabbers, the ones who live there 12 months a year through the temperature, maybe amount to 150 to 200. The population swells up, especially during the winter when snowbirds come from Canada to enjoy the warmer weather. There are people who come back every year because they like the lifestyle. There are transients.

"THIS IS A PART OF AMERICA THAT PEOPLE AREN'T AWARE OF. THESE ARE THE 0.1% OF THE POPULATION."

— BOB ZAHN

while I wasn't paying them, I would give them a four-by-six inch copy. I bought a portable printer and paper and I would make prints so they would get something in return, which they enjoyed. Afterwards, instead of just being a portrait project, it evolved into something more, a documentary, as I went back and asked everyone their thoughts on Slab City. The answers are so diverse—from the comical to the very serious—that they tell the story of Slab City. I'm not telling it. They are.

JD: What else can you tell me that this project means to you?

BZ: I'm revealing a community from the inside that is rarely seen. There are filmmakers who come in and have made films about it, but this is a still photographic series on the people there. It really gives a good picture of who they are both in photos and in comments, and I also do photographs of the landscape there. It's still not complete, but it's a very comprehensive look.

American Gothic Revisited is my statement as an artist in photographs, as a series, as a collection of who I am. I believe there's an honesty in it

JD: Where in California is Slab City?

BZ: It's east of the Salton Sea, about 20 miles southeast of Bombay Beach and north of Calipatria, where I live, then Brawley, El Centro and Mexicali. The people in Slab City are satisfied with their lives. They're there because they choose to be. Most are either unemployed or retired, others are self-employed handymen. And there's no rent, so that helps them economically. Also no building can be attached to the earth. They all have to be portable.

JD: What do you hope to accomplish by sharing it?

BZ: I think this story needs to be told. This is a part of America that people aren't aware of. These are the 0.1% of the population.

JD: Would you like to add anything?

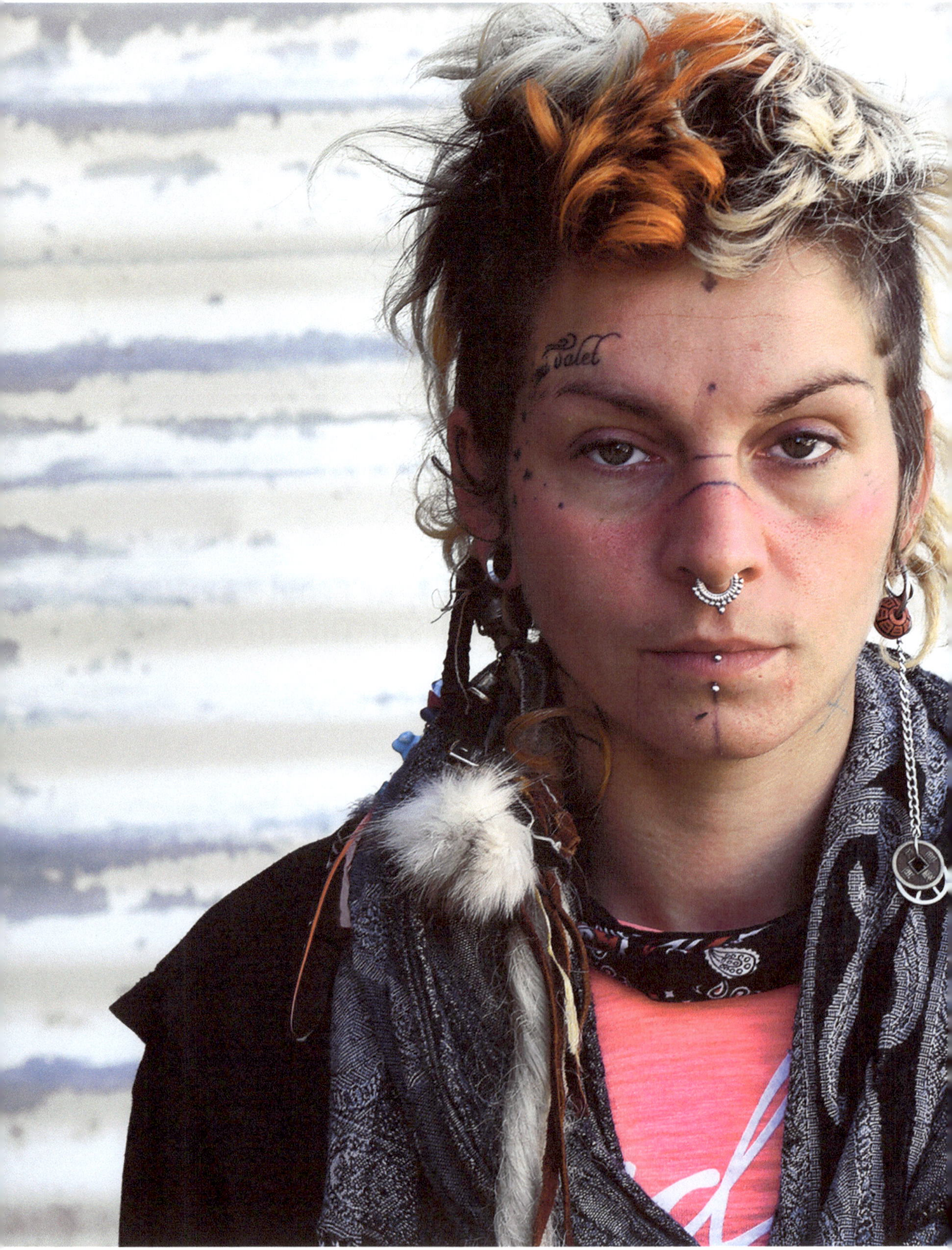

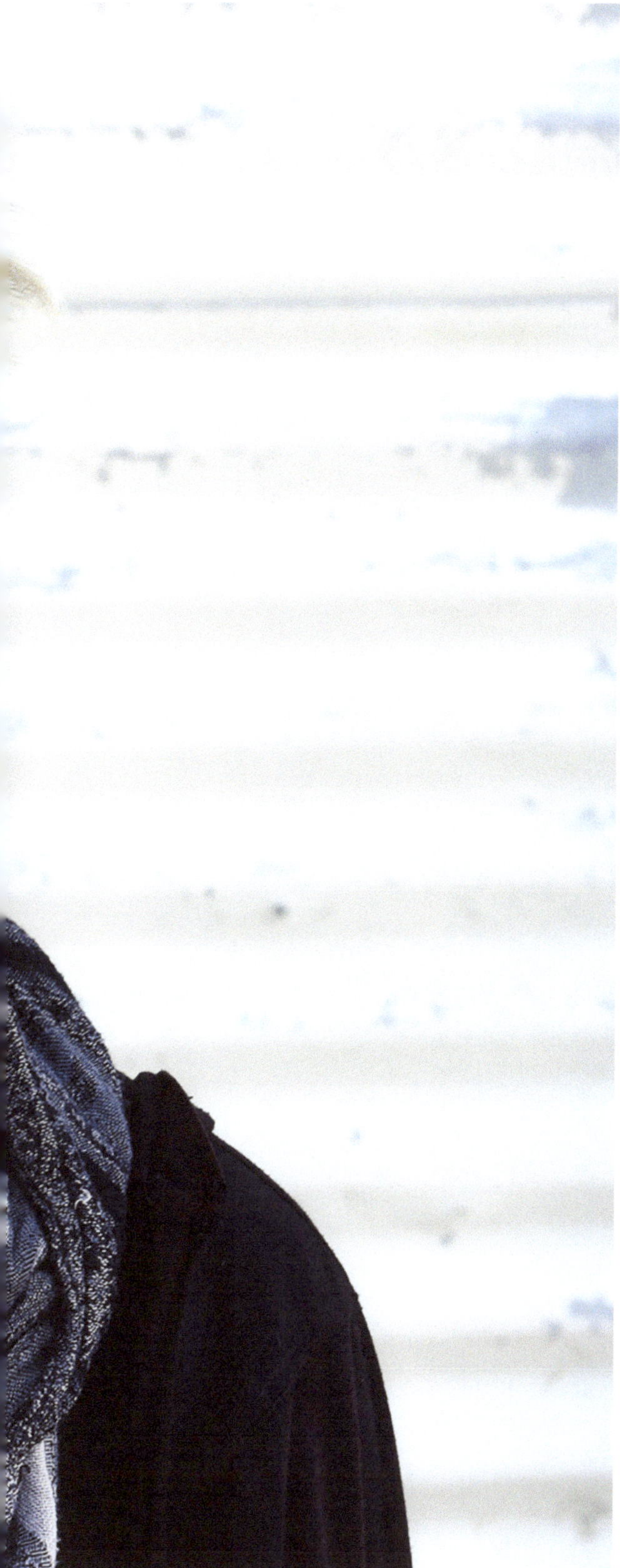

BZ: When I showed up in Slab City, I was a stranger walking into a place unknown. I have this Mamiya RZ67 Pro II film camera and a light meter. I'm over 39 years old. They were very understanding, given that only a dozen of the hundreds I photographed said I couldn't take a picture. They knew I was serious about my work. I was so serious that I started hanging out there. And I think that is what drew me into the community. I like it there.

JD: You gained their trust. That's what it takes to do an inside story.

BZ: Yes, and this is what is different from other stories about Slab City: I was there. I was seeing it from the inside. I was accepted. People opened up to me, and I opened up to them. It was a great living experience. Slab City is 180 degrees from where I grew up, where I attended school and where I used to live in New York. There's a two-lane highway through Slab City. The land is flat and 126 feet below sea level. You can see the stars at night. People are honest and real. This is a total change in my lifestyle, and I wanted it. I think the life I led in New York was dynamic, but this was a break that I needed from that life. I'm glad I found it.

'Jinx', Seasonal Slabber, *"You don't know peace until you've had suffering."*

"I WAS THERE. I WAS SEEING IT FROM THE INSIDE. I WAS ACCEPTED. PEOPLE OPENED UP TO ME, AND I OPENED UP TO THEM."

— BOB ZAHN

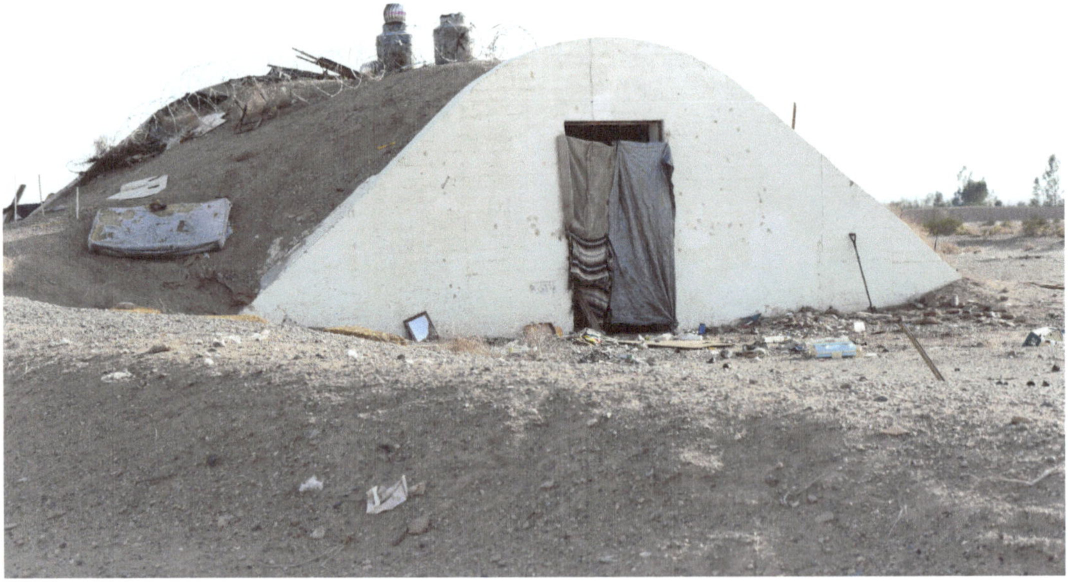

ABOVE - Bunker 1, *Former underground military fortification used to house munitions at Camp Dunlap, now occupied by Slabbers.*

RIGHT - 'Little Bear', Seasonal Slabber, *"Life is a gift. Freedom is a choice."*

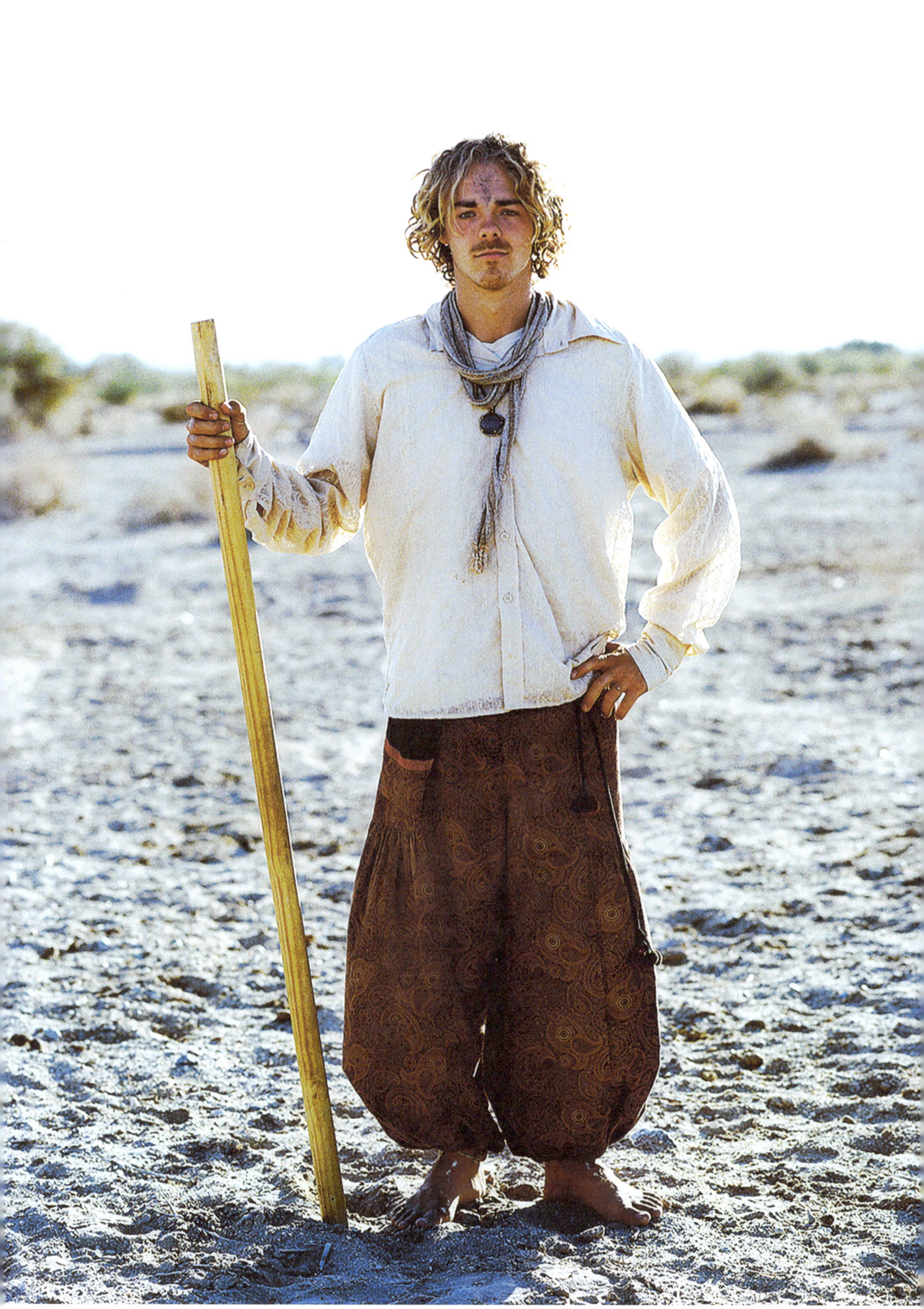

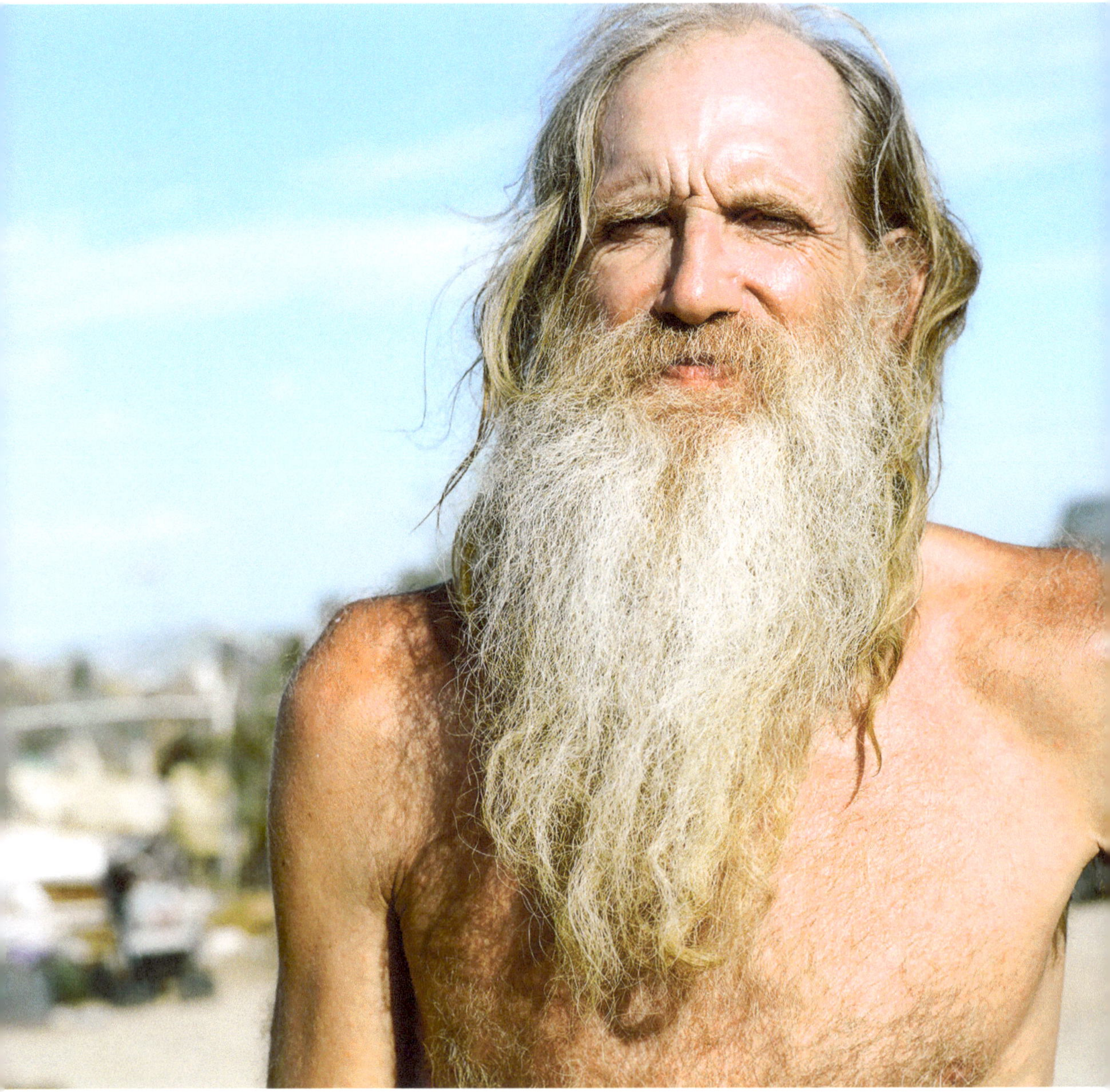

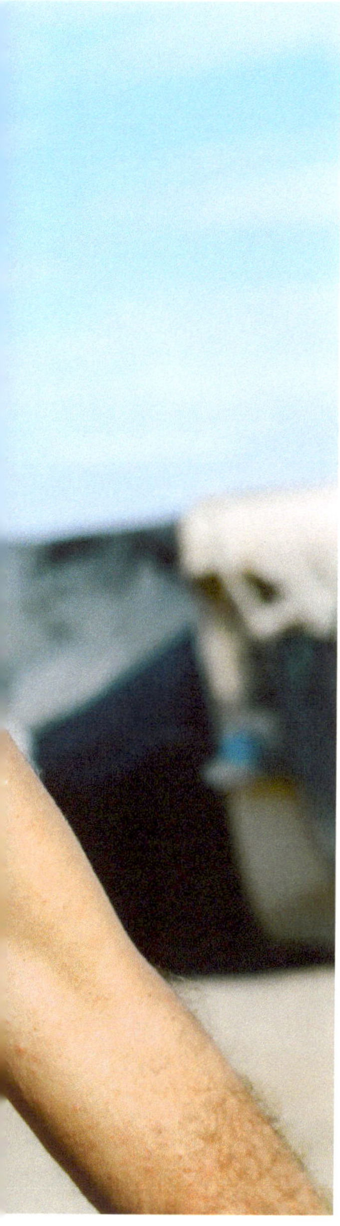

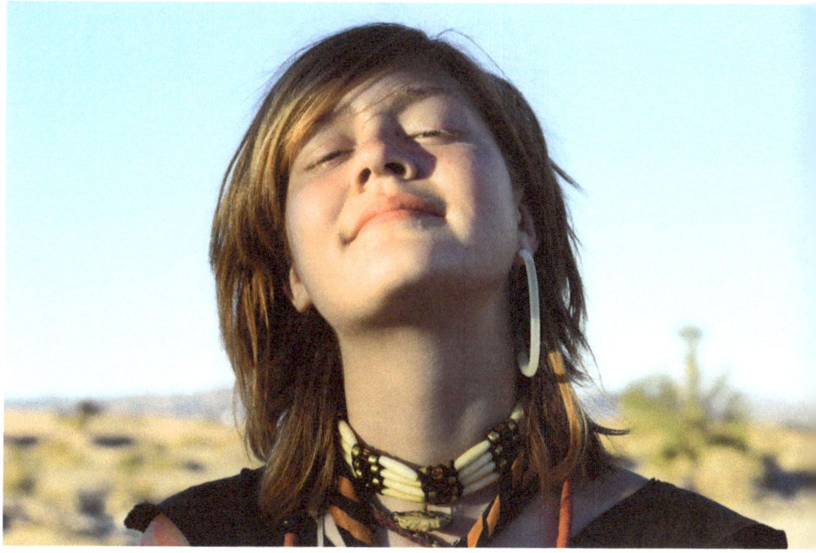

LEFT - 'Preacher Dave', Slabber, *"I was called to Slab City by God."*

ABOVE - 'Bing', Seasonal Slabber, *"No matter the amount of negativity you're presented, five minutes from now could be your best moment."*

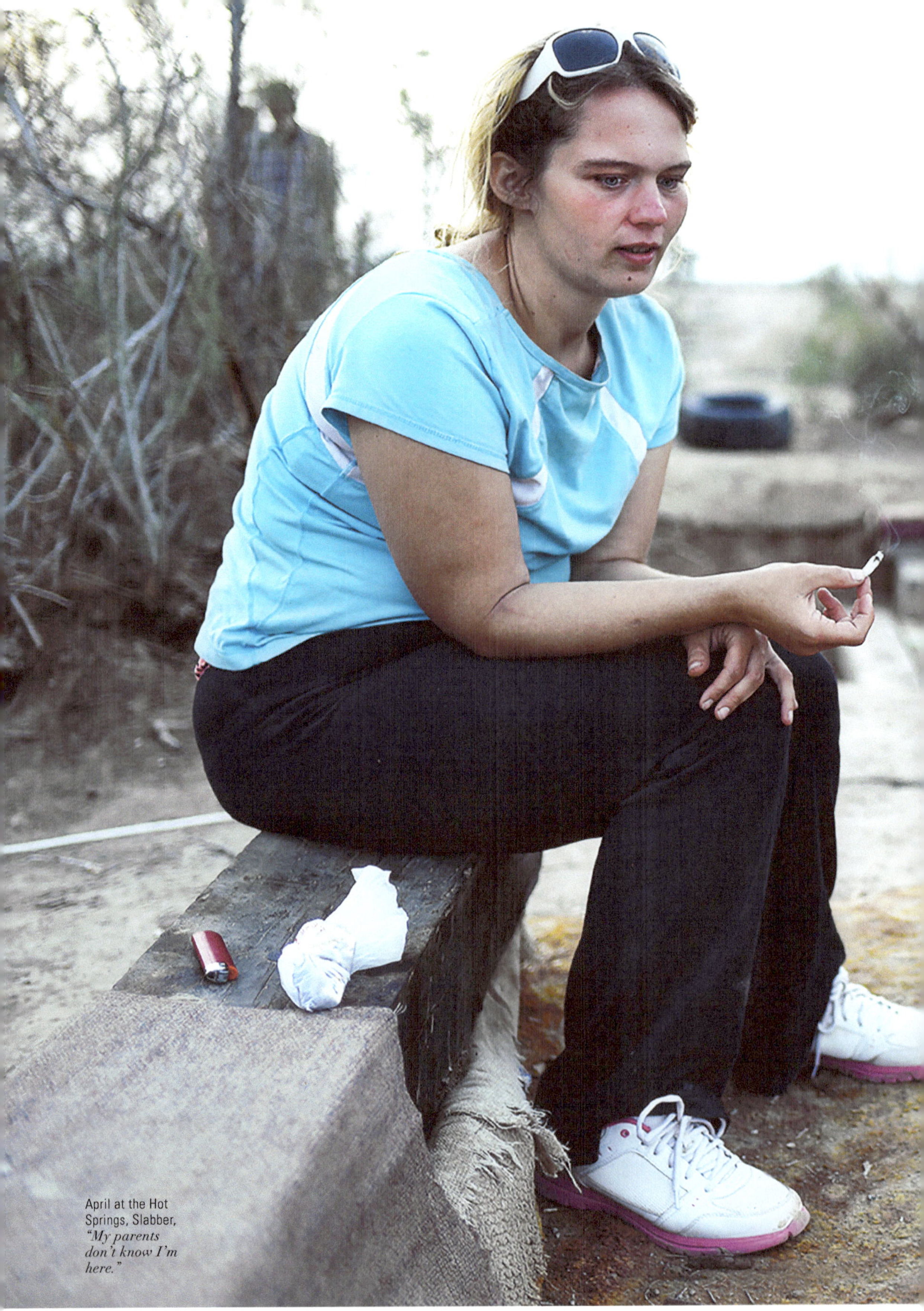

April at the Hot Springs, Slabber, *"My parents don't know I'm here."*

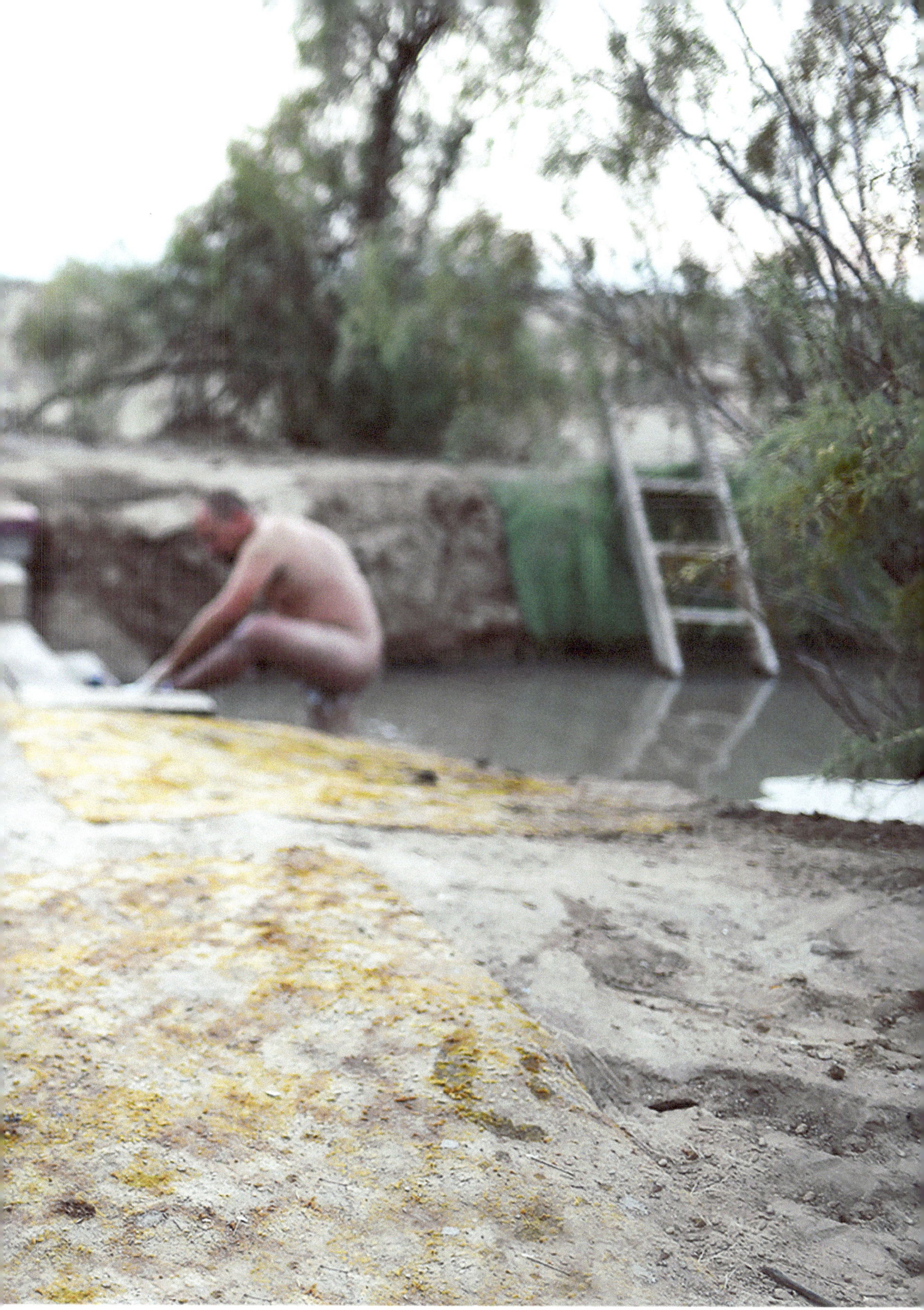

"I'M NOT PUTTING ON ANY AIRS. I'M JUST LETTING THE PEOPLE FLOW THROUGH THE LENS."

— BOB ZAHN

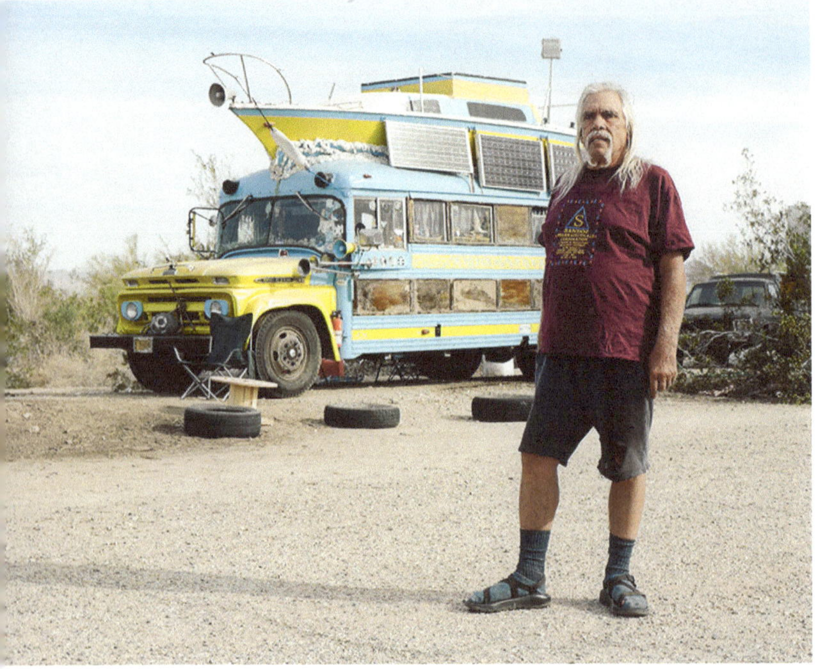

ABOVE - 'Just Mark', Seasonal Slabber

RIGHT - 'Conner', Transient

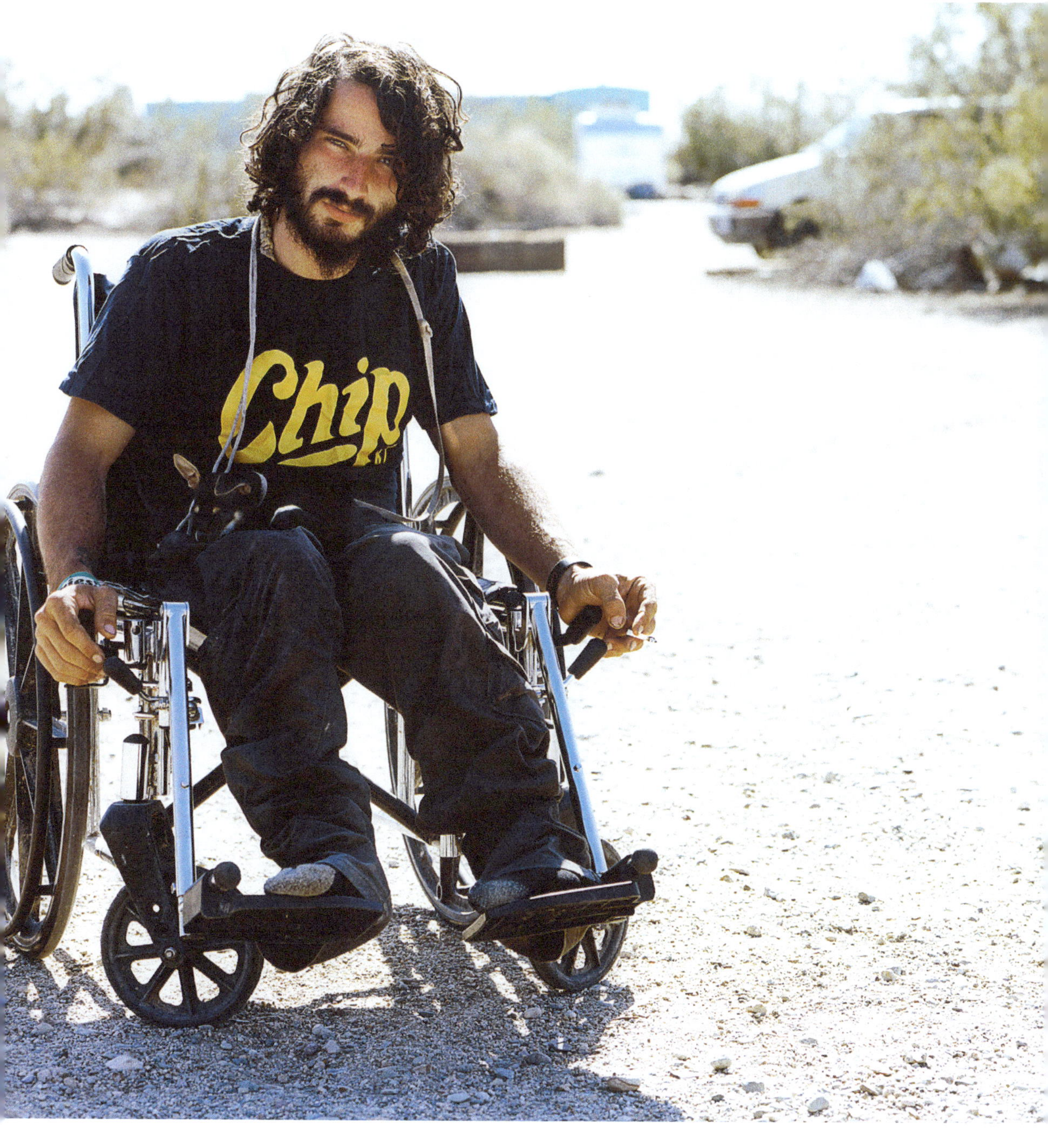
Chip

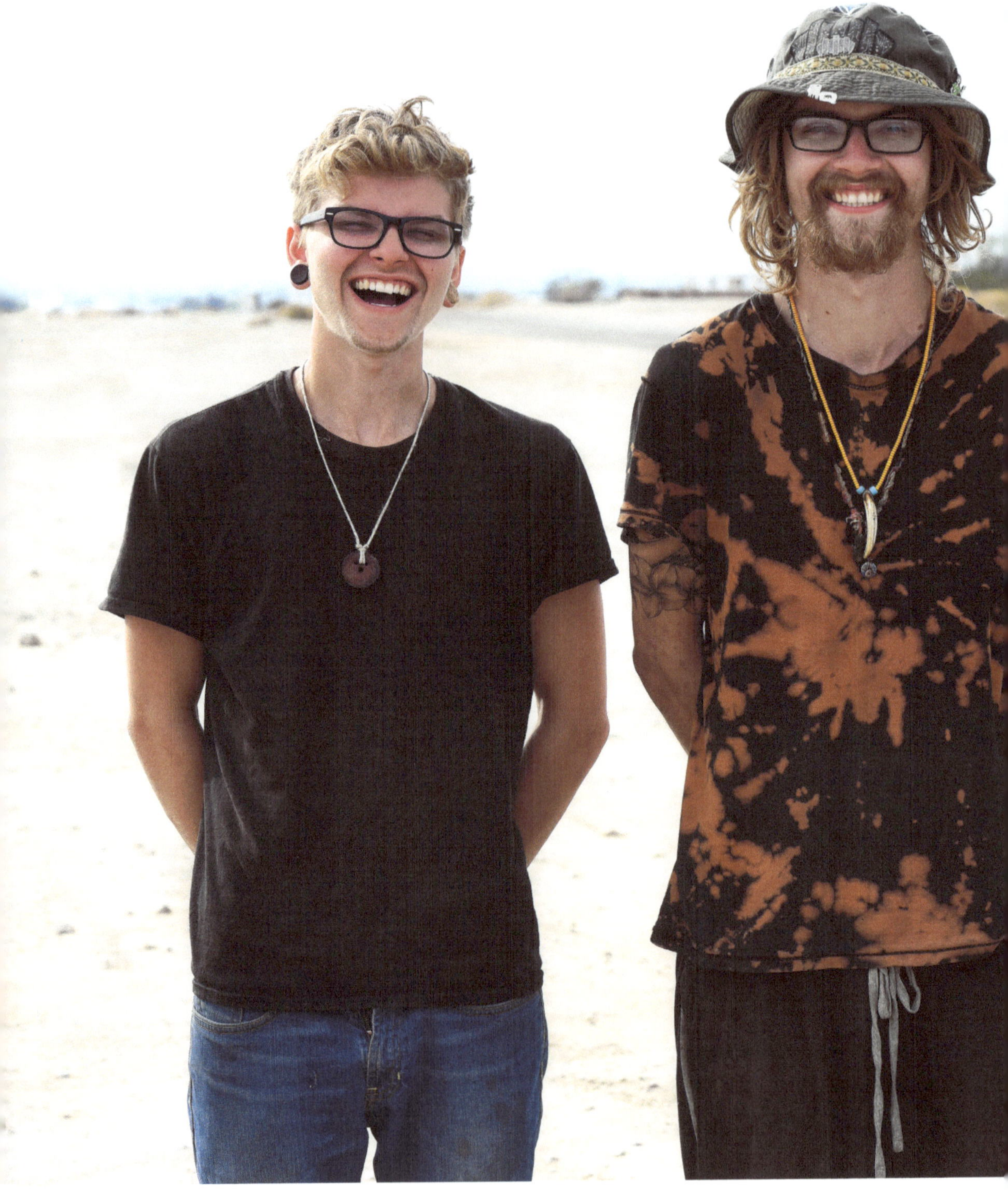

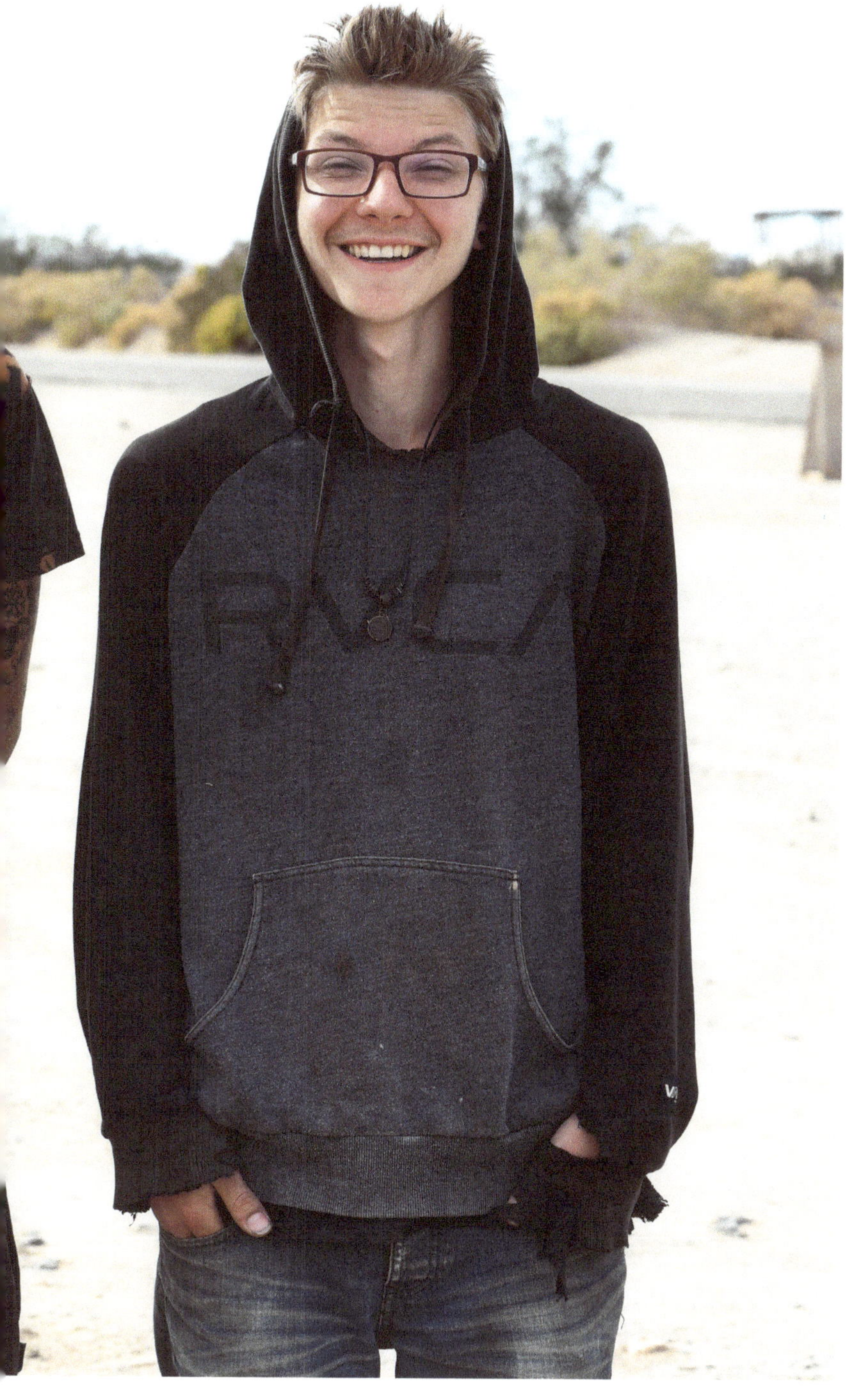

'Pilser', Brian and 'Surfer' Dave, The Hansen Brothers, Seasonal Slabbers

To Slab City, October 21, 2014: "Slab City is my favorite town in America. A desert utopia built on the remnants of war bonds. It survives as the last vestige of freedom in America, or as close as you will ever get to it. The freedom to exist. It doesn't ask you for any money to be there. It imposes no time limits. It asks only that you respect those around you and please dispose of your trash properly. Slab City is what you make of it. For me it is a place to dance like no one is watching. All those clothes you thought you had to wear are suddenly overdressed. Its a place to totally relax and reset. There is a natural hot springs to relax and bath. An underground shower, The Range for free concerts every Saturday. No place else can you communally coexist like this. In my home life on Long Island we never hung out with our neighbors, let alone 30 a day! When I am in Slab City I start my day at the Oasis Club from 7-10 chewing the fat around the table with the old timers who know a hell of a lot more than I do, I call it Life College. From 10-1 I eat some food, read a bit, sun tan perhaps. Then its an afternoon bike ride, a visit to some camps. Maybe an afternoon car to Niland 6 miles down the road for supplies at Maze market and bottle returns for beer money, picking up some hitchhikers along the way I recognize from around the fire barrels on Range night. Purchase a 6 pack of tall boy miller, the champagne of beers, for 3.69 with the money I collected on my bottle returns on the way in, fill up water jugs behind the gas station, and its back to the Slabs. Now its 5 or 6, time to eat some dinner and make it over for acoustic night, or a pot luck social, or a card game, or some other get together someone mentioned during the day... rinse repeat. Each day there fills up fast and just when you think there is nothing to do there is lots and lots to do. There are good and bad parts of the neighborhood, mostly GOOD. Want a nice safe quadrant then stick to the south west of the grid of streets, and there is a map and streets with names. There are a few clubs in town, The Oasis is the most liberal and Loners on Wheels (LOWS) is for singles only and strictly enforced so zip it up cowboy! Travelin Pals is a third club you can join. Believe me, this place can be the nicest place around, don't believe the hype and see for yourself. It will change your life."

— **Michael Kroll**, aka 'Long Island Mike'

"Your photographs speak of the work of both Edward Curtis and Diane Arbus ... the Slab City denizens live on a higher plane because they have chosen to not emulate the rich, the famous or the fashionable. It is beautiful to experience the "road not taken" that each has formulated for themselves. There's a lot to be said for following one's own heartbeat, oblivious to the stares and the snickers. Curtis because the subjects seem like old souls of an ancient tribe. Arbus because the viewers are gently coerced into recognizing the beauty inherent in "freaks."

— **Catherine Hazard**

"Good photographs expose us to metaphors, chide us with doubts and wonder, or make us ponder the nature of our existence and purpose. They compel us to question our place in the world."

— **Brett Erickson**, photographer

Rear cover: Portrait by **Robert Primes, ASC.**

FOR INFORMATION ON PURCHASING FINE ART PRINTS AND BOOKS, GALLERY EXHIBITIONS AND REPRESENTATION CONTACT THE ARTIST: BOB ZAHN: BOB@BOBZAHN.COM

www.ingramcontent.com/pod-product-compliance
Ingram Content Group UK Ltd.
Pitfield, Milton Keynes, MK11 3LW, UK
UKHW061028310726
14090UKWH00027B/359
* 9 7 8 0 9 7 4 5 1 2 4 7 1 *